A Savings Plan

HEINLE CENGAGE Learning

Y|S|G A YBM COMPANY Young & Son Global, Inc.

How do you save money?

Contents

Vocabulary

plan

save

chores

earn

rake

laundry

Lisa's Problem

Lisa's friend Brian is going to have a birthday party on Saturday.

Lisa wants to buy Brian a book that costs seven dollars.

She only has three dollars.

On Sunday

Lisa makes a savings plan.
Every day, she will do chores to earn money.
If she saves the money, she will have
enough money to buy the book.

Lisa's Savings								
Sunday								
Monday								
Tuesday								
Wednesday								
Thursday								
Friday								

Day

0 1 2 3 4 5 6 7 8

Dollars

On Monday

Lisa washes the dishes.

Her mother gives her one dollar.

She puts the money in her piggy bank.

Lisa's Savings

Day	0	1	2	3	4	5	6	7	8	9	10
Sunday											
Monday											
Tuesday											
Wednesday											
Thursday											
Friday											

Dollars

On Tuesday

Lisa takes out the trash in the evening. She earns one more dollar.

Lisa's Savings

Day	Dollars
Sunday	
Monday	
Tuesday	
Wednesday	
Thursday	
Friday	

0 1 2 3 4 5 6 7 8 9 10

Lisa's neighbor asks her to rake the leave

He gives her three dollars.

Lisa uses one dollar to buy a lollipop.

Lisa's Savings

Day	0	1	2	3	4	5	6	7	8	9	10
Sunday											
Monday											
Tuesday											
Wednesday											
Thursday											
Friday											

Dollars

Lisa does the laundry.
She earns two more dollars for doing a good job.

Lisa's Savings

Day	0	1	2	3	4	5	6	7	8	9	10
Sunday											
Monday											
Tuesday											
Wednesday											
Thursday											
Friday											

Dollars

On Friday

Lisa takes all the money out of her piggy bar
She has nine dollars.
Now she can buy the book!

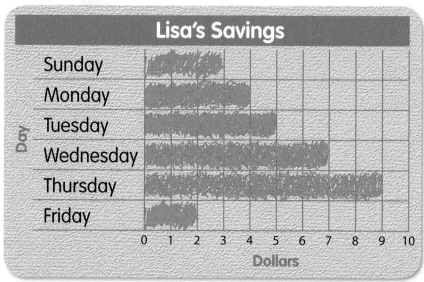

Lisa's Savings

Day	Dollars
Sunday	
Monday	
Tuesday	
Wednesday	
Thursday	
Friday	

0 1 2 3 4 5 6 7 8 9 10

Dollars

Lisa gives Brian the book and wishes him a happy birthday.
Her plan worked!

What does Lisa do to earn money?

Read a Bar Graph

A **bar graph** uses bars to compare amounts or numbers of things.

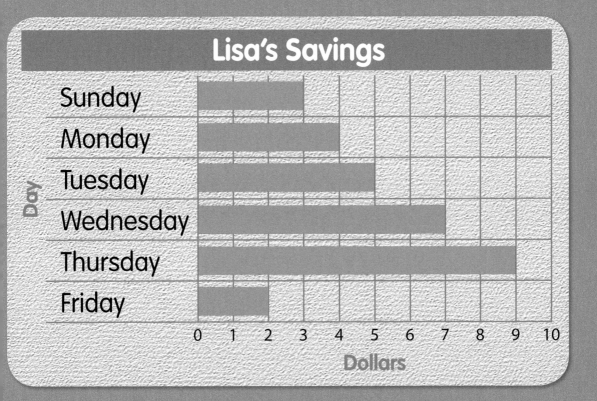

Lisa's Savings

1. On which day does Lisa have four dollars?

2. How much money does Lisa have on Wednesday?

3. On which day does Lisa have the most money?

Glossary

chore
A small job that needs to be done regularly

earn
To get money for work that you do

neighbor
Someone who lives near you

plan
Something that you intend to do and have prepared for

problem
Something that causes trouble or difficulty

save
To keep something, especially money, for use in the future

Index